I0829387

THE SPIRITUAL REFLECTIONS OF THE SUFI FREEMASON VOL.1

By SALMAN S. SHEIKH

THE SPIRITUAL REFLECTIONS OF THE SUFI FREEMASON VOL.1

COPYRIGHT 2020 © BY SALMAN S. SHEIKH – Revised in 2025

Paperback ISBN: 9798551824404 – **HardCover ISBN –** 9798284471661

Cover Art/Page also by Salman S. Sheikh. The cover consists of my personal picture. The Masonic symbol and the Sufi Crescent Heart symbol are universal symbols found in commons public resources and not copyrighted by anyone. These symbols are universal and can be used by all. The Kindle E-Book version cover is created with Amazon KDP cover art creator with allowed materials/artwork.

Any questions or comments please email me at SalmanSheikh911@gmail.com. Thank you!

Table of Contents

Introduction

Peace be upon you. Welcome to a journey not merely across the pages of a book, but through the chambers of the soul. This is more than a manuscript—it is a mirror, a map, and a message. It is the weaving together of two great spiritual legacies: Sufism, the mystical heart of Islam, and Freemasonry, the philosophical brotherhood born of ancient stone and modern light.

My name is **Salman S. Sheikh**, and this book is born not from theory, but from lived experience—written in the ink of longing, memory, and revelation. It is both testimony and tribute to the paths that have shaped me, both as a man and as a mystic.

Raised between worlds—Pakistan and America, tradition and modernity—I have always existed in the in-between. As a child, I memorized verses from the Qur'an while watching American cartoons. I bowed in prayer facing Mecca, and then stepped outside into a culture driven by individualism and noise. This duality became my teacher. It taught me to look for unity in contradiction, harmony in paradox.

Over time, I was drawn to the esoteric—the inner meanings behind words, symbols, and gestures. I found myself questioning surface-level narratives and seeking the hidden threads that connect seemingly disparate traditions. It was then that I encountered Freemasonry, and later began to understand the deeper currents of Sufism that had always surrounded me in family, culture, and ancestral echoes.

Both paths captivated me. Both demanded inner work. Both insisted on integrity and personal transformation as the price of admission.

Freemasonry presented itself not as a religion, but as a sacred architecture of the soul. Through symbolic ritual, moral allegory, and fellowship, it carved out a space where men of all creeds could refine themselves into builders—not of empires, but of virtue.

Sufism, meanwhile, whispered secrets through poetry and silence. It taught me that proximity to God is not earned through power or knowledge, but through love, surrender, and the annihilation of the self. I learned that the Beloved is not far, but veiled by our distractions.

This book, then, is the fruit of years spent walking both paths. It is a conversation between my inner selves—a tapestry of lessons from Masonic degrees, Sufi gatherings, letters to royalty, moments of stillness, and bursts of divine clarity. I share these reflections not as a master, but as a fellow traveler, a brother, a seeker who still stumbles, prays, questions, and builds.

In these pages, you will find:

- **Personal accounts** of transformation, including my spiritual correspondence with Queen Elizabeth II;

- **Historical and symbolic bridges** between Freemasonry and Sufism, from their emphasis on sacred geometry to their shared language of light, ascension, and inner labor;

- **Expanded spiritual journals**, meditations, and letters that span continents and contemplations;

- **Reflections on the universality of wisdom**, exploring how traditions as distant as Buddhism and Masonry echo each other when one listens with the heart.

This book is not meant to convert or convince. It is meant to awaken.

If you are already on a spiritual path, may this text deepen your walk. If you are unsure where you stand, may it open your heart to sacred possibilities. If you come from a tradition different from mine, may you find resonance in our shared human yearning for truth.

There is something dangerous and liberating in the message of unity. Dangerous, because it threatens the systems built on division. Liberating, because it offers the only real peace: the peace of knowing we are not separate.

You are not asked to believe. Only to listen. Not with your ears, but with your soul.

I have stood in both mosque and lodge. I have danced with dervishes and sat in solemn Masonic ritual. I have seen God in the silence of a mountain dawn and in the eyes of a stranger. And I have come to believe that our religions, philosophies, and brotherhoods are not walls, but windows—if we allow them to be.

So welcome, dear reader, to this sacred space. It is not linear. It spirals, like the Sufi's dance, like the spiral staircase in Solomon's temple. It invites you inward, always inward.

Here, you will not be lectured. You will be initiated—not with ceremony, but with truth.

Come as you are. Bring your doubts, your wounds, your hopes. There is room here.

Let us begin. <u>Please read this till the end to understand. I represent myself only.</u>

Chapter 1: Dual Paths, One Light

At the heart of every authentic spiritual path lies a call to transformation. Not superficial change, but deep, enduring alchemy. The kind that turns stone into sanctuary, ego into emptiness, and separation into union. This is the sacred work of both the Sufi and the Mason—two seemingly distant paths, yet reflections of the same eternal Light.

Imagine, if you will, two seekers born in different lands. One wears robes dyed by the deserts of Arabia, his lips whispering *Zikr* beneath the stars. The other stands in a lodge in Scotland or Pennsylvania, clad in apron and white gloves, reciting oaths under candlelight. Though their garments differ, their posture is the same: humble, reverent, inward. Each one seeks the Source. Each one builds the soul.

Sufism, rooted in the mystical dimension of Islam, is often called the "path of the heart." It is a journey through spiritual stations (*maqamat*) and divine states (*ahwal*), where the ego (*nafs*) is stripped layer by layer until only the Beloved remains. The Sufi is not content with ritual alone. He seeks direct experience—*ma'rifah*, gnosis. He cries not for heaven, but for God Himself.

Freemasonry, meanwhile, arises from the stone-cutting guilds of medieval Europe and evolves into a philosophical system of personal development, ethics, and enlightenment. The Mason begins as a rough ashlar—an unshaped stone—and through labor, discipline, and ritual, becomes the perfected self. The lodge is the temple; the tools are symbolic; the goal is light.

To walk both paths is not to be torn in two—it is to see with both eyes open.

I remember my first Masonic initiation vividly. Blindfolded, I entered the lodge as an outsider, symbolically in darkness. Yet I was welcomed as a brother, led not by sight but by trust. The symbolism was immediate: to find the light, one must surrender. To see clearly, one must first be made humble.

I had seen this before—in the Sufi circle, where the newcomer sits silently at the feet of the Sheikh, saying little, listening deeply, waiting to be changed by love rather than logic.

What struck me most were the **shared virtues**. Humility. Service. Charity. Inner purification. In the Qur'an, we are told that "God does not change the condition of a people until they change what is in themselves." Freemasonry echoes this, teaching that the true temple is not built of stone, but of virtue, justice, and wisdom.

In both traditions, **ritual is not performance—it is transformation**. The Mason is "raised" through degrees of insight. The Sufi "ascends" through stages of self-annihilation and divine love. Each degree, each station, is a death to illusion and a rebirth into clarity.

Consider the Sufi phrase: *"Die before you die."* Consider the Masonic principle: *"To be raised."* These are not metaphors. They are mystical truths encoded in ritual, meant to awaken what lies dormant within.

And then, there is **silence**.

In the lodge, silence is sacred. It is respected, guarded. It allows the heart to speak when words fall short. The same is true in the Sufi gathering, where the most profound moments happen between breaths—where the Name of God fills the room not through volume, but through presence.

There is a sacred geometry to both paths. The **Ka'ba**—the cube toward which Muslims pray—reminds us of structure, direction, stillness. The **Masonic temple** likewise orients the Mason toward East and Light. Both spaces are symbolic of the **inner sanctum**, the chamber of the heart where the divine speaks.

To understand this unity, one must abandon the surface. Do not ask whether the rituals match word for word. Ask instead whether the fruits are the same. Do they produce patience, compassion, integrity, humility? If yes, then you are witnessing the same seed blooming in different soil.

I have been asked often: "How can you walk both paths? Aren't they contradictory?"

To this I reply: contradiction is a matter of perception. Unity is a matter of essence. The Divine is not limited by names, forms, or traditions. Truth is vast. It wears many robes. It speaks in many tongues.

What matters is not the label you wear, but the light you carry.

As I deepened in both disciplines, I discovered that **the true enemy of spiritual progress is not contradiction, but compartmentalization.** We try to divide the sacred into neat boxes—religious, philosophical, spiritual, practical—as if the soul recognizes such boundaries. But the soul is whole. It sees through veils.

Sufism gave me the fire—the burning love that consumes the false self. Freemasonry gave me the form—the structure to channel that fire ethically into the world. Together, they forged in me not perfection, but commitment. A commitment to keep refining, questioning, building.

This chapter, then, is not merely an introduction to two traditions. It is a **mandala**—a pattern of harmony. It is an invitation to see beyond surface differences and into the shared archetypes of the human quest for meaning.

Whether you are a Sufi or a Mason, or neither, I ask you only this:

- Do you seek truth beyond convenience?

- Do you believe character is more sacred than dogma?

- Do you long for a world where love outweighs ideology?

If so, then welcome. You have already begun the work.

You are the seeker. You are the stone. You are the sanctuary.

And the light you seek? It is already within you—waiting to be uncovered, remembered, raised.

Chapter 2: Letters of Spirit and Sovereignty

There are moments in life that defy logic and speak directly to the soul—moments that seem stitched into reality by divine hands. One such moment for me began with a letter. Not just any letter, but one addressed to the Sovereign of the United Kingdom: Her Majesty Queen Elizabeth II.

What prompts a man—a Pakistani-American Sufi Freemason—to write to a monarch? Faith. Reverence. And the hope that words, when written with truth and humility, can transcend borders, bloodlines, and history.

The act of writing that letter was not political. It was profoundly spiritual.

I had been reflecting on the state of the world—on rising divisions, spiritual confusion, and the deafening loss of dignity in public discourse. I felt compelled to reach out across what most would call an impossible divide. With sincerity, I wrote about the values that still matter: justice, mercy, compassion, unity. I spoke of my faith. Of my grandfather. Of Freemasonry and Sufism. Of our shared humanity.

I did not expect a reply. Yet, one came. Then another.

The Queen's responses were formal, yes, but they were also gentle, timely, and filled with the quiet grace that power often forgets. In those words I found something rare: recognition—not of me as an individual, but of the universality of what I was expressing.

It was a reminder that truth speaks not to titles, but to hearts.

But the truest monarch I ever knew was not crowned. He wore no medals. He held no throne. His name was **Mian Muhammad Shareef Sheikh**—my grandfather.

He ruled with wisdom, not decree. His realm was a village called Sukho Chak, nestled near the volatile borders of pre-partition India and Pakistan. And during the cataclysm of 1947—when nations were drawn with colonial pens and soaked in blood—he chose peace.

British soldiers, once the colonizers of our land, found themselves vulnerable and hunted during the chaos. My grandfather did not seek revenge. He offered protection. His village, his people, became a sanctuary not just for Muslims, but for the human spirit.

That is sovereignty.

True sovereignty is not control. It is conscience. It is the ability to rise above vengeance and choose dignity.

He made sure his village became part of Pakistan—securing not only land but legacy. His vision ensured that generations, including mine, would live in relative peace. His decision wasn't calculated. It was guided—by faith, by integrity, by the quiet strength that comes only from inner alignment.

In Freemasonry, we are taught that the ruler of the self is greater than the ruler of nations. That the Master Mason is not the one who commands others, but the one who governs his own passions. My grandfather lived this truth before I ever read it in a ritual.

In Sufism, the greatest leaders are not those who wield power, but those who disappear into service. The Sheikh is not glorified; he is emptied. So that the Divine may work through him, unimpeded.

My grandfather was both. Sheikh in blood. Mason in spirit.

So too were my parents sovereigns of a quieter, hidden kingdom.

My father, **Shafiq Sheikh**, did not rule a village. He ruled his schedule—sixteen-hour workdays in a foreign land to provide for his children. He did not speak often. But when he did, it mattered. His hands, calloused and tired, built not monuments, but futures.

My mother, **Naseem Sheikh**, was my first prayer, my first teacher, my first sanctuary. Her strength was subtle, yet absolute. She taught me the sacredness of patience, of compassion, of unconditional love.

If the world could be run by such souls—mothers who nurture without reward, fathers who sacrifice without recognition, grandfathers who lead without ego—we would need no kings or queens.

In their honor, I wrote to a Queen. But in truth, my letters were always addressed to something higher: the Sovereign Spirit that lives in us all.

As a Freemason, I believe in the Grand Architect of the Universe—a Creator who designs not buildings, but character. As a Sufi, I seek intimacy with the Divine—a Lover who asks not for rituals, but for remembrance.

Both paths taught me to write letters that matter. Not just with ink, but with life.

Each choice we make is a letter. Each act of mercy is a petition to the unseen. Each moment of integrity is a sealed envelope addressed to eternity.

So write, dear reader. Write with your breath. Write with your hands. Write with the echo of your ancestors guiding your steps.

The sovereign you are meant to be does not reside in palaces. He lives in your courage. She lives in your compassion. And together, they rule not others—but yourself.

This chapter is about correspondence, yes. But not only of paper and pen. It is about the greater correspondence between heaven and earth, between our deeds and our destiny.

To write is to believe your voice matters. To govern is to live like it does.

Chapter 3: Ancestral Echoes and Earthly Pillars

Behind every spiritual seeker stands an unseen crowd.

They are not always saints or scholars. Some never prayed aloud, never wrote a single verse. Yet their footsteps are the ones we follow. Their voices echo through our conscience. Their decisions, often made in silence and sacrifice, are the unseen blueprints of the temple we now inhabit.

This chapter is about those silent architects. The ancestors whose names may be forgotten by history—but whose impact lives in the structure of our lives.

In Freemasonry, we are taught that the Temple of Solomon was constructed not merely with stone, but with intention. Each pillar, each beam, each measurement—divinely ordered. The same is true of our families. Our ancestors, knowingly or not, carved the space in which our souls now awaken.

In Sufism, the connection to lineage is more than biological. It is spiritual. We speak of the *silsila*—the chain of transmission from master to student, heart to heart. It is believed that when a Sufi begins his path under a true Sheikh, he is not walking alone. He is accompanied by a river of light stretching back to the Prophet himself.

And so, when I speak of ancestry, I do not mean mere heritage. I mean the **spiritual DNA** that pulses through our every act of goodness. I mean the unseen blessings—*barakah*—that follow us not because we earned them, but because someone before us prayed we'd receive them.

Let me begin with the **pillar of my foundation**: my grandfather, **Mian Muhammad Shareef Sheikh**.

I remember the stories told about him. Not fables, but living truths. As a respected village chief during the Partition, he was entrusted with not just land, but lives. When others chose revenge, he chose protection. When others demanded division, he chose unity.

One of the most profound legacies he left was not in land, but in ethics. He taught me that real strength is measured by restraint. That a true leader is not the loudest voice, but the calmest presence in the storm. That one moment of mercy can outlive centuries of fear.

I often wonder what was in his heart when he made those impossible decisions. I imagine he did not see himself as a hero. Just a man doing what conscience demanded. And yet, in that moment, he became a **pillar**—not just in our family, but in the architecture of peace.

Then there is my father, **Shafiq Sheikh**. If my grandfather was the foundation, my father was the builder. Brick by brick, shift by shift, dollar by dollar, he constructed a life for his children. He didn't ask for thanks. His love was not loud, but it was unwavering.

There's something deeply Masonic about his ethos. Freemasonry teaches that labor—when done in silence and integrity—is sacred. My father embodied this. He woke before dawn, returned after dark, and rarely spoke of his exhaustion. He did not sculpt marble, but he shaped futures. And in doing so, he reminded me that every honest effort is a prayer.

My mother, **Naseem Sheikh**, was the heart that made our house a home. Her softness did not mean weakness. Her gentleness was a force. She infused our lives with warmth, prayer, and protection. Where my father built with hands, she built with spirit.

She taught me what the Sufis call *rahmah*—mercy. That compassion is not passive. It is revolutionary. It is the unseen thread that holds families, communities, and civilizations together.

In every moment of doubt, I have returned to her example. In every act of love I offer to others, her fingerprints remain.

And then, there are the ancestors whose names I do not know—those buried under forgotten stones, whose dreams became our inheritance.

I imagine them watching. Smiling. Hoping.

In Freemasonry, we speak of **those who have gone before us**, whose work we continue. In Sufism, we honor the saints, the righteous, and the seekers of truth who paved the way.

But I believe each of us has saints in our bloodline. Some were never recognized. Some lived and died in silence. Yet their prayers reached the heavens. Their sacrifices were recorded in the Divine register. And their light reaches us still.

This chapter is not just about honoring the past. It is about realizing that **we are now the ancestors of the future**. What we build will be inherited. What we neglect will become someone else's burden.

To honor your ancestors is to live in such a way that they would be proud.

To become a true spiritual builder is to ask: What am I leaving behind?

A Freemason carves with discipline. A Sufi loves with abandon. A true human being lives so that others may breathe easier tomorrow.

As you read this, think of your own pillars. Who labored so that you could read this book in peace? Who sacrificed so you could sit in safety? Who whispered prayers over your sleeping form?

Honor them. Live for them. Build with them in mind.

And know that your legacy begins not when you die, but with every choice you make now.

Chapter 4: Masonic Brotherhood and Sufi Orders

Brotherhood is a word often romanticized yet rarely understood. In the world of hashtags and hollow pledges, it is easy to forget what true fraternity looks like. Brotherhood is not simply about shared identity or loyalty. It is about shared transformation. About meeting others at the threshold of becoming, walking with them through fire, and emerging forged—not by blood, but by choice.

Freemasonry and Sufism are both built upon this rare and sacred type of brotherhood. One bound not by doctrine, but by discipline. Not by uniformity, but by unity of purpose.

My first experience entering a Masonic lodge was not about robes or regalia. It was about presence. The quiet dignity of men gathered in solemn intention. The gravity of the ritual. The awareness that this was not a performance—it was a gateway.

The man who sat beside me in silence, who shook my hand with reverence, became a brother not because we shared the same religion or ethnicity, but because we were willing to build something greater than ourselves—together.

Later, when I sat at the feet of a Sufi Sheikh in Pakistan, I felt the same energy. There was no applause. No spotlight. Only the presence of transmission—heart to heart, breath to breath. My brothers in the *khanaqah* (spiritual retreat house) came from all walks of life. Some were farmers. Others scholars. Some carried visible wounds; others bore invisible ones. But all came to dissolve the self, to know the Divine.

This is the sacred fraternity: to walk with others not to be seen, but to be changed.

The Lodge and the Sufi Circle

The Masonic lodge and the Sufi circle are two sanctuaries that mirror one another more than most realize.

In the lodge, the initiate begins in darkness, symbolically blind, dependent on his guide. He is led step by step through degrees that represent not just stages of knowledge, but transformations of being. He learns to work on the temple within, to shape his character as a builder shapes stone.

In the Sufi path, the *mureed* (student) is led by the *murshid* (guide). He, too, is blind—not in sight, but in insight. His nafs (ego) clouds his vision. The Sheikh, like a Master Mason, reveals not secrets, but selfhood. Through daily *zikr* (remembrance), discipline, and love, the disciple ascends spiritual stations—each one a degree, each one a death to illusion and a birth into divine intimacy.

The lodge and the *zawiya* are spaces of structured transformation. The rituals differ in form but align in purpose: to reveal what is real.

Symbols, Secrecy, and Sacred Language

Both Freemasonry and Sufism are often misunderstood because of their use of symbolism and secrecy.

But secrecy, in these traditions, is not about exclusion. It is about reverence. The sacred cannot be shouted. It must be whispered. Protected. Lived.

The Masonic square, compass, and plumb line are not merely tools of architecture. They are instruments of moral measurement. The Sufi's prayer beads, cloak, and staff serve similar functions—not as artifacts, but as signs pointing inward.

The language of both traditions is poetic, metaphoric, and multilayered. Just as the Mason studies allegory to uncover truth, the Sufi reads verses and hears echoes— meanings layered like the concentric circles of a rose.

In both, the true initiate is not the one who has memorized the most, but the one who has transformed the most.

Equality on the Path

In the Lodge, you meet on the level. In the Sufi order, you bow before none but the Divine.

I have seen professors sit beside janitors in both settings. I have seen CEOs humbled by the presence of a dervish. These are not anomalies—they are the rule. Because when you truly seek truth, titles fade. When you approach the Beloved, only sincerity remains.

This equality is not political—it is spiritual. It is rooted in the understanding that the soul has no hierarchy. That God does not rank men by their resumes, but by the openness of their hearts.

Tested Through Trial

One of the most profound shared realities of both orders is the concept of trial.

In Freemasonry, the initiate is tested—not for the sake of challenge, but purification. He must prove himself faithful, honest, dedicated. He must keep the secrets, not to hide truth, but to protect the process of revelation.

In Sufism, trials come in the form of loss, longing, loneliness. The path to the Beloved is not linear. It spirals. It burns. The disciple is stripped of falsehood. He is shown his shadow before he is shown the Light.

Brotherhood, then, is not about comfort. It is about companionship in the crucible.

The Hidden Hand of Love

At the heart of both traditions lies one power: love.

Not romantic love. Not conditional love. Divine love.

The Mason builds with it. The Sufi burns with it. And through that love, both are transformed.

I remember a moment in lodge where a brother, weeping silently during a closing charge, gripped my hand after we stood. No words. Just a look of recognition. I've seen that same look in the eyes of dervishes spinning in ecstasy, of seekers lost in the rhythm of *zikr*.

It is the look of those who have touched something real.

One Brotherhood, Many Names

The world loves labels. It craves division. But the soul sees unity.

You may call yourself a Freemason. A Sufi. A Christian. A Buddhist. A seeker.

It doesn't matter.

What matters is this: Are you building? Are you loving? Are you remembering?

If so, then you are already a member of the only true order—the eternal fraternity of the Spirit.

Chapter 5: Bridging Realms Through Ritual

There are things in this world that cannot be explained, only experienced. A well-executed ritual is one of them.

It is a sacred choreography of spirit and symbol—a living language that speaks not to the mind but to the soul. Ritual is how the unseen becomes felt, how truth becomes embodied, and how the human being becomes the temple of the Divine.

Both Freemasonry and Sufism understand this at the deepest level. They know that a truth heard is soon forgotten, but a truth enacted is carved into the marrow.

Ritual, when sincere, is a bridge. A bridge between the outer and inner, the material and mystical, the temporal and eternal.

The Architecture of the Sacred

In Freemasonry, the lodge is laid out with geometric precision. Every object has purpose. Every movement is symbolic. The East represents wisdom, the West strength, the South beauty. These are not decorations—they are coordinates for spiritual orientation.

The initiate enters blindfolded, in darkness, symbolic of ignorance. His journey is marked by knocks, words, grips, and oaths. Each element has been refined over centuries—not to obscure, but to unveil.

Likewise, in Sufism, the circle of *zikr* is no mere assembly. The order of sitting, the sequence of invocation, the rhythm of the breathing—all are divinely designed to open the heart's inner chambers.

When the *mureed* begins the litany—"La ilaha illa Allah"—he is not simply repeating a phrase. He is recalibrating his being, realigning every cell to the vibration of truth: There is no god but God.

The Power of Presence

True ritual demands presence. Not the body's, but the soul's.

You cannot fake your way through a Sufi *hadra* (spiritual invocation) without being felt. Nor can you recite Masonic charges with robotic detachment and expect them to land.

Presence is what animates the form. Without it, ritual is performance. With it, ritual is portal.

I have been in lodges where silence was more eloquent than speeches. I have sat in Sufi gatherings where a single tear carried more weight than an hour-long sermon.

These are the places where heaven bends down to kiss the earth.

Silence and Sound: Two Doors

Ritual is built on opposites: sound and silence, stillness and motion, concealment and revelation.

In Freemasonry, silence is not an absence—it is an instruction. Before speaking, the initiate learns to listen. Before leading, he learns to obey. There is a sacred discipline in the pauses between words, a deeper language in the unsaid.

Sufism, too, balances this duality. While *zikr* can be loud, even ecstatic, there are other moments of absolute silence, of *muraqabah*—watchfulness. Here, the Sufi listens not with ears, but with the soul.

In both paths, sound is the flame, but silence is the wick.

Death, Rebirth, and the Alchemy of Repetition

Repetition in ritual is not redundancy. It is alchemy.

When the Mason traces the same symbols, utters the same oaths, and walks the same path, he is not going in circles. He is spiraling—deeper, higher, inward.

When the Sufi repeats the Name, over and over, it is not mindless. It is heart-full. Each repetition polishes the mirror of the soul until, one day, it reflects only the Beloved.

And at the center of both traditions is the greatest ritual of all: death and rebirth.

The Mason is symbolically "killed" and then "raised" as a Master. This is not theatrical. It is mystical. He dies to the profane and is reborn to the sacred.

The Sufi speaks of *fana*—the annihilation of the ego. And *baqa*—the subsistence in God. He dies before dying, so that he may truly live.

These are not fantasies. They are invitations.

The Sacred in the Ordinary

Ritual teaches us to see the sacred not just in temples, but in life.

After enough degrees, the Mason begins to see the square and compass in everything—his speech, his relationships, his work. After enough *zikr*, the Sufi begins to hear God in birdsong, in traffic, in silence.

Ritual is not a destination. It is a lens.

Through it, you begin to live differently. With intention. With reverence. With awareness that the world is not mundane—it is mystical.

Protecting the Fire

But ritual is fragile. It can become routine. It can lose its fire.

This is why both traditions stress **intention**. The Sufi calls it *niyyah*. The Mason hears it in every charge to upright conduct.

Without intention, even the holiest ritual becomes performance. With it, even the simplest act—washing a dish, lighting a candle—becomes holy.

The ritual is not what changes you. Your sincerity within it does.

Ritual as Resistance

In an age of speed and distraction, the very act of slowing down, of gathering in silence, of moving with sacred purpose, is radical.

To invoke the Name of God with intention is to rebel against nihilism.

To memorize a charge or chant a sacred verse is to say: I believe in more than profit. I believe in mystery.

This is why our rituals are under threat—not from critics, but from forgetfulness.

We must protect them—not as relics, but as living fires.

You Are the Ritual

Ultimately, the greatest ritual is your life.

You are the temple. You are the circle. You are the sacred act unfolding moment by moment.

Walk like your steps are prayers. Speak like your words are offerings. Work like your labor is part of the Grand Design.

The world does not need more beliefs. It needs more initiated souls. More men and women who live as bridges—between tradition and modernity, between inner and outer, between self and Source.

So build your altar. Light your candle. Say your words.

And then… become them.

Chapter 6: Buddhism and the Mystic Path

There is a silence in the teachings of the Buddha that echoes across millennia—a silence that does not ask for belief, but invites awareness. A silence that is not empty, but pregnant with presence. It is in this sacred stillness that I discovered a resonance so profound, it startled me: the teachings of Buddhism, though born in the East under different skies, whisper many of the same truths I encountered in Sufism and Freemasonry.

This chapter is not about comparing religions. It is about listening to the same music played through different instruments. The mystic path is one path—though it wears different robes and speaks different tongues. It is the path of awakening.

The Buddha and the Builder

The story of Siddhartha Gautama, the Buddha, begins in privilege. He was born into royalty, shielded from suffering. But his soul demanded more than comfort. He left his palace, his titles, and his illusions to confront the human condition directly. What he discovered was not another doctrine, but a way—a way beyond suffering, beyond identity, beyond illusion.

This, too, is the way of the Sufi. This, too, is the journey of the Mason.

The Sufi walks away from ego (*nafs*) in search of annihilation (*fana*), not because the world is evil, but because only by letting go can one see clearly. The Mason, too, must shed his old self, must be "initiated," must labor to transform the rough ashlar into a temple of light.

Like the Buddha, we are not called to escape the world, but to transcend it through understanding, compassion, and clarity.

The Noble Truths and the Divine Blueprint

Buddhism begins with Four Noble Truths:

1. Life is suffering (*dukkha*).

2. Suffering is caused by craving and attachment.

3. There is a way to end suffering.

4. The way is the Eightfold Path.

The Sufi would agree. Suffering is the veil that awakens the soul. The *nafs*, our unpurified ego, is the source of attachment. And the cure is not escape, but surrender.

The Mason, too, acknowledges the imperfection of life—and seeks to build not in rebellion against suffering, but through it. Every stone, every lesson, every trial is a sacred blueprint drawn by the Great Architect of the Universe.

The Eightfold Path in Buddhism—right view, intention, speech, action, livelihood, effort, mindfulness, and concentration—is echoed in Masonic moral instruction and Sufi ethical refinement.

Meditation and Muraqabah

One of the most well-known Buddhist practices is **meditation**—stilling the mind, watching the breath, observing thought without clinging. This practice builds awareness, compassion, and detachment.

The Sufi equivalent is *muraqabah*—a state of spiritual watchfulness. The seeker sits in silence, not to empty himself, but to become a vessel. He watches his thoughts, his breath, his desires, and lets them go. He tunes his inner being to the frequency of Divine Presence.

Freemasonry, while less focused on formal meditation, still creates sacred space for inner reflection. The quiet moments in a lodge—between the charges, oaths, and degrees—are filled with the same invitation: go inward.

Stillness, across traditions, is the sanctuary of awakening.

The Bodhisattva and the Sheikh

The **Bodhisattva** is a being who, though capable of achieving final liberation (*nirvana*), chooses to stay behind in the realm of suffering to help others awaken. He walks with one foot in heaven and one in the world. His compassion is boundless.

This is precisely the function of the Sufi Sheikh—the guide who has walked the path, tasted the union, and now lowers his hand to lift others. He does not instruct with pride, but with love. His very presence is medicine.

In the Masonic tradition, the **Worshipful Master** holds a similar role—not as a dictator, but as a spiritual craftsman guiding others through symbolic rebirth and ethical refinement.

Each tradition recognizes that **true mastery is found in service**, and that the highest power is not domination, but compassion.

Non-Attachment and the Mystic's Freedom

Buddhism speaks of **non-attachment**—not to life, not to pain, not even to joy. This is not apathy. It is freedom. The Buddha teaches that clinging is suffering. To love without possession, to give without demand, to exist without identification—this is liberation.

The Sufi understands this deeply. He loves with his whole being, yet demands nothing. He serves with his hands open. He chants the name of God not to earn favor, but to dissolve into Him.

The Mason, too, learns to circumscribe his desires. To work not for reward, but for the harmony of the Great Work.

This is a freedom that no empire can grant. It is the sovereignty of the soul.

The Middle Way and the Perfect Balance

The Buddha spoke of the **Middle Way**—a path between indulgence and denial. It is the golden mean. The balanced life.

Freemasonry teaches the same: moderation in all things. Discipline, not dogma. Honor, not harshness.

Sufism teaches *wasatiyyah*—a Quranic principle of balance and harmony. The Sufi avoids extremes. He is not an ascetic hermit, nor a worldly hedonist. He lives in the world but is not of it.

Truth, they all agree, is not found in excess. It is found in stillness, in balance, in the space between.

Universal Brotherhood and the Oneness of All

Buddhism sees all beings as interconnected. The illusion of separateness is the root of violence. To awaken is to see clearly: that your enemy is you in another form, that every act of kindness ripples across the cosmos.

Sufism echoes this through the concept of *wahdat al-wujud*—the Unity of Being. There is no separation, only veils.

Freemasonry enshrines **universal brotherhood** as its cornerstone. Race, religion, class—these are irrelevant in the Lodge. What matters is character, sincerity, and the shared goal of building a better world.

These traditions do not simply preach tolerance. They embody unity.

The Initiation of Existence

To be born is to be initiated. To suffer is to be refined. To love is to be enlightened.

Whether you sit beneath a Bodhi tree, spin in a Sufi circle, or kneel in a Masonic lodge—if you are seeking, refining, remembering—you are already walking the mystic path.

It is not the label that matters. It is the **labor**.

Breathe. Observe. Chant. Build. Love.

And in the sacred silence between heartbeats, listen…

That is the Divine, calling you home.

Chapter 7: Journal of Reflections

There are places the intellect cannot go. Places where only the heart can travel—where the soul speaks not in arguments or doctrines, but in sighs, silence, and sacred symbols.

This chapter is a map of those places.

What follows are excerpts from my personal reflections, captured in moments of stillness, sorrow, gratitude, and revelation. These entries are not polished prose or philosophical treatises. They are the honest echoes of a soul in progress.

They are prayers with punctuation. Footsteps in ink.

March 1, 2018 – The Letter I Never Sent

Today I wrote a letter I never mailed. It was addressed to God. Not in the formal way—no "Dear Creator" or "Oh Lord Most High." I simply wrote, "Are You still listening?"

And I waited.

There was no thunder. No lightning. Just a breeze.

But somehow, I knew.

Yes.

June 12, 2018 – Between the Apron and the Heart

Tonight I wore the apron again. Entered the lodge with steady breath. The ritual was flawless. But what struck me was the moment after—when we sat in darkness, waiting for the light.

That silence is everything. It is the breath before creation. The moment before truth is spoken.

I wish more people knew this peace.

October 27, 2018 – The Rose and the Mirror

Sitting in *muraqabah* today, I had a vision: a mirror placed before a rose.

But the mirror was clouded. The rose—breathtaking. I understood that the rose was God, and I was the mirror.

My job is not to reach the rose. My job is to reflect it—clearly.

January 1, 2019 – New Year, Same Soul

Everyone around me made resolutions. Lose weight. Make more money. Travel.

I made one too: *Feel everything more deeply.*

Pain. Joy. Loss. Love. Even boredom.

Because to feel fully is to live fully. The mystic path is not about escape. It's about immersion.

April 14, 2019 – When My Ego Died (Again)

I said something cruel today—sarcastic, sharp. I saw the other person's face collapse. And in that moment, I saw my *nafs* laughing.

How easily we wound others with cleverness.

Later that night, I wept in prayer. Asked God to break my ego again. And again. Until only kindness remains.

August 30, 2019 – At the Grave

Visited my grandfather's grave. No fanfare. Just earth, stone, and silence.

I knelt down, placed my hand on the soil, and whispered, "I'm trying."

I think he heard me.

November 11, 2019 – Night Lodge in London

There's something about the air in an English lodge. The weight of tradition. The echoes of rituals done centuries ago. Tonight, as I stood among brethren of many faiths, I felt what unity truly is.

Not sameness. But sincerity in shared intention.

The ritual ended. But the presence remained.

March 3, 2020 – Sufism in a Coffee Shop

A barista today said, "You look like a monk." I smiled. Told her, "Only on the inside."

But it made me think—perhaps the truest mystics don't wear robes. Perhaps they just carry stillness.

May 6, 2020 – The Weight of Words

I taught my little cousin how to say "SubhanAllah"—Glory be to God.

Later, I heard him whisper it to himself while watching ants move in perfect order.

It humbled me. He saw the miracle. I had forgotten.

Children are closer to the truth than we are.

September 14, 2020 – Solitude is a Sanctuary

I used to fear being alone. Now I crave it.

In solitude, there are no masks. No posturing. Just me, and the Presence.

And that is enough.

December 24, 2020 – The Whisper

Tonight, during silent *zikr*, I heard a whisper—not with my ears, but in my soul:

"You were never alone."

It broke me. In the best way.

February 22, 2021 – The Light in Her Eyes

My mother was ill today. Her breathing slow. Her words soft.

But in her eyes, I saw the strength of ten thousand prayers.

This woman carried me through storms I never even noticed. She is my first lodge.

My first mosque. My first sacred space.

April 9, 2021 – Temple of Breath

Each inhale is a prayer. Each exhale, a surrender.

Breath is ritual. And my body is a temple.

If I treat it as such, every moment becomes worship.

July 19, 2021 – My Brother's Tears

A brother in lodge cried tonight. Silently. During the Third Degree.

I didn't ask why. I just placed my hand on his shoulder.

Sometimes, presence is the answer.

October 1, 2021 – The Dance

Watched dervishes whirl in Konya. Lost all sense of time.

They weren't dancing. They were becoming.

I whispered to myself, "God spins too. Around every atom."

Conclusion of Reflection

These entries are not about me. They are about us.

The sacred is not just in ancient texts. It's in the coffee shop. The hospital bed. The gravesite. The silence between friends. The ritual beneath breath.

You do not need to be a scholar to be a mystic.

You just need to be present. And honest. And willing to feel.

Write your own journal. Not for publication. For revelation.

You are not just reading a book.

You are writing one—with your life.

Chapter 8: Universal Lessons of the Spirit

There comes a moment in every spiritual journey where words fail. Where rituals give way to silence, where books are set aside, and the seeker is left only with what he has become.

This chapter is that moment.

Here, I step away from the specific languages of Sufism and Freemasonry and speak in the universal tongue—the language of spirit, soul, and sacred remembrance.

These lessons are distilled from tears, prayers, failures, and fleeting glimmers of divine grace. They are not rules. They are reflections. Not dogma, but direction.

If they resonate, it is not because I wrote them, but because you already knew them.

1. The Divine is Closer Than Breath

You do not need to climb mountains to find God. You do not need to fast for forty days or read ancient scripts in archaic tongues. God is where you are. Now. Here.

In the Qur'an, it is said, *"We are closer to him than his jugular vein."*

In Buddhism, it is known that *nirvana is not found—it is realized.*

In the Masonic tradition, the light is never imposed—it is revealed from within.

Stop running. Be still. The Beloved is already within you.

2. Purify, Then Beautify

The Sufi cleanses the heart like a mirror. The Mason refines the self like a stone. The Buddha sweeps the mind like a temple.

Spiritual life begins with **removal**: of arrogance, greed, distraction, falsehood.

Only then can the virtues emerge. Truth. Humility. Patience. Joy.

Don't rush to adorn your soul. First, make it a worthy home.

3. Presence is the Path

You can chant all the divine names, memorize all the verses, know all the degrees—but without presence, it is noise.

Real worship is not about volume. It is about **attention**.

The Sufi says: "Worship God as if you see Him."

The Buddhist says: "When drinking tea, only drink tea."

The Mason, in ritual, is taught to "pay attention to every sign, word, and gesture."

Live like this. Eat, walk, speak, and breathe with presence.

4. The Work is the Worship

Stop searching for holy ground. You are standing on it.

The act of raising your child with love, the way you greet your neighbor, how you handle someone's anger—this is your ritual.

In Sufism, everyday acts can become sacred through *niyyah* (intention).

In Masonry, labor itself is divine when done uprightly.

The mystic path is not about escaping the world. It's about infusing it with reverence.

5. Love Without Condition

All paths agree on one truth: love is the highest law.

But not love that expects something in return.

Love that heals. Love that sees. Love that forgives again. And again. And again.

This is the love of the Bodhisattva, of the Sheikh, of the true Master Mason.

You are not asked to agree with everyone. Only to love them.

6. Accept Your Shadow

You are not only light. You have shadows. Wounds. Darkness.

Don't deny them. Know them.

The ego, the *nafs*, the pride—these are your greatest teachers.

They are not obstacles. They are invitations to transform.

Freemasonry teaches you to "know thyself."

Sufism teaches you to "die before you die."

Buddhism teaches you to "observe, not identify."

Self-awareness is not shame. It is liberation.

7. Serve Quietly, Generously, Joyfully

Don't wait for applause. Or recognition. Or reward.

Sweep a floor. Hold a door. Feed a stranger. Smile when no one's looking.

This is true sovereignty.

Service is not beneath you. It is your crown.

8. Know That All Traditions Point Home

The symbols may differ. The prayers may sound different. The rituals may vary.

But listen closely. Beneath it all, they are saying the same thing:

"Awaken. Love. Return."

Don't fight over the names of God. Bow to what they mean.

9. Live Your Truth Softly

You don't have to convert the world.

Be the sermon. Be the temple. Be the peace.

Let people feel something sacred in your silence.

10. Keep Building

You are not finished. You never will be.

Every day is another stone in the temple.

Every act of truth is another beam.

You are not here to be perfect.

You are here to be **true**.

And truth, my brother, my sister, my seeker—

Truth is light.

Conclusion: The Final Degree

So here we are—at the edge of the written word, at the end of this offering, and yet, at the beginning of something far more important: your journey.

If you have made it this far, you are not simply a reader. You are a builder. A seeker. A soul stirred by mystery, love, and the call of the unseen. This book may close, but the path it points to never ends.

I have written of temples and tombs, of aprons and rosaries, of Queenly letters and ancestral prayers. I have led you through rituals, across borders, and into silence. But none of this matters—not truly—if it remains outside of you.

Because the final initiation does not happen in a lodge or a shrine. It happens within. When the heart cracks open in love. When the ego surrenders. When your hands begin to build what your soul believes.

This is the Final Degree.

Not conferred by men. Not sealed with symbols. But lived—hour by hour, breath by sacred breath.

Remember This

You are the Temple. Every choice you make lays another stone.

You are the Flame. Every act of truth makes it burn brighter.

You are the Prayer. Every moment of silence echoes through the heavens.

Remember Them

Remember the ancestors who walked before you—who bled, wept, and worked so you could be free.

Remember the mentors, the brothers, the mystics who reminded you of your light.

Remember the strangers who showed you mercy.

And remember the Divine, who has never once forgotten you.

The World is Starving for Spirit

You live in a world drenched in distraction, where truth is shouted and love is sold. But you—yes, you—are different.

You feel too much. You ask too many questions. You carry a silence that confuses others.

This is your gift.

Protect it. Nurture it. Let it grow.

Because the world doesn't need more noise.

It needs more souls who have remembered.

Be the Bridge

Between East and West. Between form and formlessness. Between creed and compassion.

Be the one who prays without prejudice. Builds without ego. Loves without limits.

Be a Freemason in your ethics. A Sufi in your surrender. A Buddhist in your awareness. A Christian in your forgiveness. A human in your heart.

And when asked what you believe, smile gently and say:

"I believe in Light."

To My Brothers and Sisters

Thank you for walking this path with me. I do not claim perfection. I still stumble. I still forget. But I keep returning. To the work. To the breath. To the Beloved.

If this book has touched you, then its purpose is fulfilled. If it has awakened something in you, then I am honored.

But please—do not stop here.

Live this. Build this. Share this.

Because the Brotherhood is not a club. It is a **cosmic order**.

And we—all of us—are initiates.

Final Prayer

O Light beyond form,

O Architect beyond blueprints,

O Beloved who whispers through stone and silence—

Raise us. Refine us. Remind us.

Let our lives become sanctuaries.

Let our hearts become lamps.

Let our work become worship.

And when we return to You,

May we do so not as strangers,

But as Builders.

As Lovers.

As Lights returned to the Source.

Ameen. So mote it be.

Thank you for reading my book and sharing its teachings with others. I am still learning like yourself and I pray you were able to take something away from my message with an open mind and had patience with my grammar as this is only Volume 1 and there is always room for future editions/improvements. As Masons we are imperfect and always learning but it's the intention that counts. May God bless all of you and your families and may he make our life's journey easy as we go from one phase to another. When I pray to God, I pray for all and to see a world where everyone and their families have a chance to live in peace. Let us take the lessons in this book and apply them to our lives as we become better day by day spiritually and physically. Please remember this life is too short, take things day by day and do not hurt anyone's heart. Always be in love and peace knowing if today was my last day on this Earth, I did not do anyone wrong. As Salam Aleikum (Peace be upon you and yours.)

If you would like to contact me for any questions or comments please email me at SalmanSheikh911@gmail.com

If you would like video versions of this book please find the respective chapters by video title on my channel. www.YouTube.com/c/SalmanSheikh911

For further reading on my background:

I have several Masonic articles I have been published in as well. The first one was "Masonic Renewal" published in August 2018 by *The Pennsylvania Freemason.* The second is "The Practices of The Sufi Freemasons." By *The Rocky Mountain Mason* magazine Issue 17. The third publication is my article "The Transhumanist AI Future & Freemasonry's Place In It." By The *Southern California Lodge of Research* March 2020 edition. I also have an online article called "I Shall Return" on the *Freemason Information* blog site which details my departure and return to the brotherhood and what I learned from it. Also, check out my latest book *Parallel Teachings Of Islam, Sufism, & Freemasonry: From The Eyes Of One Who Has Seen It All.*

Glossary

Ancestry – Spiritual and biological lineage that influences one's moral, emotional, and mystical development.

Ashlar (Rough/Perfect) – In Freemasonry, the rough ashlar represents the unrefined self; the perfect ashlar represents a state of moral and spiritual perfection.

Barakah – A Sufi term meaning divine blessing or spiritual grace, often passed through righteous lineage or acts.

Baqa – The state of remaining in God after the annihilation of the self (*fana*); spiritual subsistence in Sufism.

Brotherhood – A sacred bond between individuals committed to shared spiritual or moral principles, found in both Masonic and Sufi traditions.

Circumscribe – In Freemasonry, to set boundaries for personal conduct and passions through discipline and self-control.

Compass and Square – Central Masonic symbols representing spiritual balance and ethical action.

Ego (Nafs) – The self or lower self in Sufi terminology, often seen as the obstacle between man and God.

Fana – The annihilation of the ego/self in Sufism, leading to unity with the Divine.

Great Architect of the Universe – The Masonic title for the Supreme Being, inclusive of all faiths and traditions.

Initiation – A ritual of entry into a spiritual or philosophical order, symbolizing death to the old self and rebirth into new awareness.

Inner Temple – The personal spiritual center built through discipline, devotion, and inner work.

Khilwah – Spiritual seclusion or retreat in Sufism, often used for deep inner reflection and communion with God.

Legacy – The spiritual, moral, or cultural impact left by an individual's life.

Light (Spiritual) – A metaphor for divine knowledge, truth, and awareness; central to both Masonic and Sufi paths.

Lodge – The gathering place of Freemasons, symbolizing both a physical and internal space of sacred learning.

Maqamat – Stages or stations on the Sufi path that mark spiritual progression.

Mason (Freemason) – A member of the Masonic fraternity, committed to ethical living, spiritual growth, and universal brotherhood.

Muraqabah – A Sufi meditation technique of spiritual vigilance, awareness of God's presence.

Nafs – The self or ego in Sufi psychology, which must be purified to attain divine closeness.

Qibla – The direction of prayer in Islam, oriented toward the Ka'ba in Mecca.

Ritual – A symbolic and sacred act performed to initiate, align, or transform the participant.

Sheikh – A spiritual master in Sufism who guides disciples along the path to God.

Sufi – A practitioner of Sufism, the mystical path of Islam emphasizing divine love, inward purification, and unity with the Creator.

Temple (Spiritual) – In both Sufism and Freemasonry, the sacred inner sanctuary cultivated through discipline and devotion.

Truth – The highest aim of all spiritual paths, transcending doctrine and rooted in universal principles of justice, compassion, and love.

Zikr – The remembrance of God through repeated invocation of divine names, central to Sufi practice.

References

1.   The Holy Qur'an. Translations by Yusuf Ali and Muhammad Asad.

2.   The Bible. New International Version.

3.   The Dhammapada. Translated by Eknath Easwaran.

4.   Rumi, Jalal al-Din. *The Essential Rumi*. Translated by Coleman Barks.

5.   Hanh, Thich Nhat. *The Heart of the Buddha's Teaching*. Parallax Press.

6. Pike, Albert. *Morals and Dogma of the Ancient and Accepted Scottish Rite of Freemasonry*. Supreme Council, 33°, Southern Jurisdiction, U.S.A.

7. Nasr, Seyyed Hossein. *The Garden of Truth: The Vision and Promise of Sufism, Islam's Mystical Tradition*. HarperOne.

8. Schuon, Frithjof. *Understanding Islam*. World Wisdom.

9. Guénon, René. *The Esoterism of Dante*. Sophia Perennis.

10. Shah, Idries. *The Sufis*. Anchor Books.

Bibliography

Books and Texts:

- Ali, Abdullah Yusuf. *The Meaning of the Glorious Qur'an*. Amana Publications.

- Asad, Muhammad. *The Message of the Qur'an*. The Book Foundation.

- Knight, Christopher. *The Hiram Key*. Element Books.

- Lings, Martin. *What is Sufism?* University of California Press.

- Burckhardt, Titus. *An Introduction to Sufi Doctrine*. World Wisdom.

- Kabbani, Shaykh Muhammad Hisham. *Classical Islam and the Naqshbandi Sufi Tradition*.

- Jones, Bernard E. *Freemasons' Book of the Royal Arch*. Macoy Publishing.

- El-Yasin, Norbert. *Masonic and Islamic Mysticism: A Comparative Study*. Unpublished Thesis.

Articles and Journals:

- "Mysticism and Brotherhood: Comparative Theology of Sufism and Freemasonry." *Journal of Esoteric Studies*, Vol. 17, 2021.

- "The Architecture of the Soul." *Spiritual Masonry Quarterly*, Winter 2020.

Multimedia:

- Sheikh, Salman S. *YouTube Reflections and Journal Transcripts*, 2019–2021.

- Audio lectures and interviews with Freemasons and Sufi teachers, private collection.

All content within this book is my original work and a transcript version of my YouTube video lectures. THE SPIRITUAL REFLECTIONS OF THE SUFI FREEMASON VOL.1

Extra Content , Disclaimers, Masonic Egregore –

This profound work explores the inner spiritual parallels between **Islamic Sufism** and **Freemasonry**, as experienced personally by Salman S. Sheikh —a Pakistani-American Sufi and initiated Freemason. Rather than advocating for institutional membership, the book is a spiritual reflection and esoteric testimony. It speaks from the heart, weaving autobiography, metaphysics, ritual, ancestry, and sacred universalism into one deeply personal path of self-discovery and divine connection. I have resigned honorably in good standing from Freemasonry and represent myself

only in this book.

Core Teachings and Themes:

1. **Unity of the Esoteric Path:**

- Sufism and Freemasonry are portrayed not as contradictory but as

complementary mystical systems. Both are seen as tools to polish the ego,

refine the character, and uncover divine light within.

- Both traditions use symbols, rituals, and silence to bring the initiate closer to

the Divine.

2. **Ritual as Transformation:**

- Ritual is not pageantry but **alchemical practice** that transmutes the ego into

spirit. In both traditions, death and rebirth—symbolic or real—are key to

spiritual awakening.

- The Masonic lodge and Sufi circle (zawiya) are both sanctuaries for

transformation and mirrors of divine order.

3. **The Inner Temple:**

- Freemasonry teaches building the inner temple with discipline and moral rectitude; Sufism calls for dying to the self (fana) and living through God (baqa).

- The true temple is within, constructed by the heart's sincerity and the soul's yearning for truth.

4. **Sacred Brotherhood and Compassion:**

- Brotherhood in both orders is not social but **spiritual fraternity**—a meeting of souls committed to growth.

- True brotherhood transcends race, religion, or class. Sincerity is the highest common denominator.

5. **The Sovereign Self:**

- Drawing on personal ancestry, especially his grandfather's and father's legacy, Salman S. Sheikh redefines sovereignty as **moral courage and spiritual leadership**.

- True royalty is the individual who governs his own desires and serves others selflessly.

6. **Ancestry and Spiritual Legacy:**

- The spiritual inheritance passed from elders is framed as more critical than material wealth.

- The ancestors are "pillars" in the architecture of one's inner temple.

7. **Universal Mysticism:**

- The book draws striking parallels between **Sufi**, **Buddhist**, and **Masonic** practices, asserting that all true spiritual paths seek awareness, compassion, and awakening.

- The Buddha's Middle Way, the Sufi's path of love, and the Mason's upright labor all guide toward the same Source.

8. **Journal Entries:**

- These reflections serve as vulnerable and poetic moments of spiritual intimacy.

- They document the spiritual highs and lows, from silence in lodges to visions during Sufi meditation.

9. **Final Teachings:**

- The culmination teaches that **you are the ritual**; life is the sacred ceremony.

- Build with love, serve with humility, and awaken the inner light to reflect divine presence.

Parallels Between Freemasonry and Islam (Sufism):

Freemasonry — Islamic Sufism

Grand Architect of the Universe — Allah (The One, The Real Architect)

Initiation through degrees— Ascension through maqamat (spiritual stations)

Silence as sacred — Muraqabah (watchfulness) and internal silence

Symbolic tools (compass/square) — Symbolic tools (tasbih, cloak, staff)

Inner temple building — Heart purification and annihilation (fana)

Brotherhood across lines — Universal ummah (community of love)

Allegory and ritual — Poetry, metaphors, and zikr

Emphasis on moral character — Tazkiyah (soul purification)

Freemasonry borrowed much of its spiritual architecture from **Islamic Spain**, the **Crusades**, and esoteric contacts with the East. Geometry, sacred architecture, light symbolism, and initiatic progression all echo Islamic and Sufi traditions.

Salman S. Sheikh 's Final Messages:

- **This book is not an invitation to join the lodge or grand lodge system.**

- The **lodge/grand lodge system today is corrupted by racism, politics, and ego**.

- Rather, this work is a call to **embrace the pure esoteric values already in Islam**—truth, self-purification, divine love, and service.

- Salman S. Sheikh 's allegiance is to **God, Truth, and Love**, not to institutional power structures.

Final Dedication and Free Speech Statement:

I represent myself only under the principles of free speech.

This book is dedicated to my beloved father, Shafiq Ahmed Sheikh (may Allah grant him peace).

It is not a motivation to join any Masonic lodge or grand lodge, but rather to awaken to the timeless spiritual teachings that are already enshrined in Islam.

The grand lodge system has deviated into politics, racism, and ego, and no longer represents the inner light it once sought to protect.

Let us return to **the real Freemasonry**—building the inner temple through love, truth, remembrance, and presence—ideals already perfected in **Islamic Sufism**.

<u>**Understanding the Impact of the Masonic Egregore on Your Life**</u>

First before anything — To ensure a complete separation, it is recommended that you formally resign and demit in good standing from your Blue Lodge (Craft Masonry) and any affiliated side orders or appendant bodies. This process entails ensuring all financial obligations, such as dues, are current with each organization. Initiate this by contacting the secretary of your regular

lodge and the respective secretaries or governing officers of all other Masonic bodies to which you belong. Begin by submitting your resignations to the side orders and appendant bodies first, securing your demit letters or letters of clearance from each. Once this documentation is received, you may then proceed with your resignation from the Blue Lodge. Should you encounter any difficulties or evasiveness from the secretaries or leaders at any level, it is advisable to contact the District Deputy for your Blue Lodge and the relevant leadership for the side orders to facilitate the process. Upon receiving all necessary paperwork confirming your demission and resignation from all Masonic entities, your separation will be complete. The Egregore doesn't go away if you're suspended or expelled, YOU MUST leave honorably in good standing. If you're having issues, don't let it get to a point where you can't fix it.

The Masonic Egregore is a real spiritual construct that feeds off rituals, oaths, and energy given by members. It continues to impact individuals long after physical resignation, unless consciously revoked.

Common effects of the Masonic Egregore: - Health deterioration and chronic fatigue - Sleep paralysis, nightmares, insomnia

- Financial blockages and stagnation

- Conflict in marriage, family, and friendships - Mental fog, anxiety, or spiritual numbness

- Obstruction in prayer and connection to God

The goal of the rituals is to feed the Egregore. This is why after your degrees are complete, the fraternity

largely neglects you—except when it comes to paying dues. Grand Lodges and local lodges are declining rapidly. By the mid-2030s, Freemasonry will be significantly reduced as newer generations are disinterested, especially as all the esoteric knowledge is now freely available online.

Many Grand Lodges are becoming desperate, openly encouraging people with slogans like: "Don't wait to be invited." This is a reflection of their declining influence.

When you begin your resignation process, you'll notice strange behavior: brothers become distant, social interactions vanish, and the warm fraternity you once knew fades. This is because leaving harms the Egregore, and it stops feeding off your energy. Suddenly, the messages, likes, and invitations stop. In truth, you were paying for friendship and feeding a spiritual entity with your energy.

Healing Process:

Once you follow the full revocation process laid out in this document, you begin your path to healing. To maintain and deepen your healing:

- Establish a consistent spiritual practice based on your personal path or religion. - Engage in daily prayer, dhikr, or scriptural reading.

- Stay in righteous company and avoid spiritually dark environments.

- Reaffirm your Tawhid and renunciation of false oaths.

- Seek divine light, mercy, and truth to replace past darkness.

Freedom starts with the decision to leave, but true transformation unfolds step by step, day by day.

Further Signs of Egregore Influence Within the Brotherhood:

It is important to recognize that many who remain within the system of Freemasonry begin to show noticeable signs of spiritual and physical imbalance. While this is not to condemn individuals, the pattern is revealing and deeply connected to the nature of the Egregore that feeds off low-vibrational behaviors.

Many members are observed to be:

- Chronically overweight and physically unhealthy

- Constantly hungry, both physically and spiritually, never feeling satisfied

- Addicted to drugs, alcohol, or tobacco to cope with internal emptiness

- Engaged in marital infidelity or emotional betrayal of their spouses

- Secretly addicted to pornography, masturbation, or obsessive sexual behaviors

These behaviors are not just coincidental — they are direct manifestations of spiritual bondage and disconnection from the Divine. The Masonic Egregore thrives in environments where lust, gluttony, addiction, and deception are present. These behaviors drain personal energy, feed the collective Egregore, and keep individuals locked in spiritual confusion.

Recognizing these signs is the first step toward liberation. As you break free, you may notice your appetites begin to normalize, your heart starts to soften, your mind becomes clearer, and your connection to your Creator grows stronger.

Remain steadfast. Keep purifying. And know that healing, light, and divine truth are on the other side.

All content within this book is my original work and a transcript version of my YouTube video lectures. THE SPIRITUAL REFLECTIONS OF THE SUFI FREEMASON VOL.1